I'll always Love you no matter what!

Illustrations Lavinia Trifan

Translation: Elisabeta Ivan

To ....
From Emma and Ioana,
"To as many successful experiments as possible!"
....

Coordinating editor: Florentina Ion
Copy Editor: Luminița Volintiru
DTP: Mihaela Nicolae
Counselor: Cristina Trepcea,
psychologist and psychotherapist

DIDACTICA PUBLISHING HOUSE
16 Splaiul Unirii Blvd.,
Muntenia Business Center Building,
5th floor, 506, District 4, Bucharest

www.edituradph.ro
e-mail: office@edituradph.ro
Orders and info:
Phone: +40-21-410.88.14;
+40-21-410.88.18.
Fax: +40-21-410.88.10

Copyright 2017 © Didactica Publishing House.
All rights reserved.

Emma is an adorable energetic girl, always curious, smart and beautiful, like all children. She has two lovely parents, a younger and fluffier brother, a chocolate-brown cat and lots of colorful fish in an aquarium, in the living room.

Because Emma likes to know
everything about the things in the world,
she does a lot of interesting experiments.

For example, one day she wanted to know what her things would look like if piled-up. Are her things together bigger than a small mountain? And how long would it take her to climb this mountain? When Mommy came to ask her if she had finished cleaning her room, Emma replied:

"Yes, look, me put everything
in pile-order here, on the carpet.
Look, Mommy, how clean closet is now!"

Ever since she was very young, Emma has learned from her mom and dad that they both love her up to Jupiter and back and that their love will never disappear, no matter what happens.

Although Emma knows that mommy and daddy never tell lies, she wants to make sure.

So, she always asks her mom or dad if they still love her when she does less pleasant, unusual or even dangerous things, which she calls "experiments".

Every single time, they take her in their arms, look her in the eye and say in the warmest voice in the world: "I will always love you, no matter what you do, my little planet of joy!"

One day, Emma was very eager to taste the cat's crunchy croquettes. Emma knew that people don't eat dry food for cats, but she was craving. When mommy was busy vacuuming and the cat was sound asleep on a backpack, she approached the bowl with croquettes on all fours, took a whole fist and stuffed them in her mouth.

She tried to chew them, but they were not as she had imagined. They were very hard, salty and oily so she quickly went to the bathroom to spit them in the sink.

Then her stomach ached all day, but her soul ached even worse when she saw her mother's disappointed face:

"Emma, have you eaten any of the cat's croquettes? I see some bits around your mouth ..."
"Mommy, but me not eat them! Me just wanna be sure they are delicious, so cat not eat something bad to taste. But, you were right, they are not good at all. What strange tastes cats have!"

Another time, Emma really wanted to feel on her skin what "hot" really means. So, she stuck her finger in the polenta which was recently poured out from the caldron, even though Mommy had told her hundreds of times not to get near anything from which steam came out.

"Ouuch!" she shouted and ran to mommy to ease her pain.

Mommy quickly took Emma in her arms, applied a special burn solution on her finger, rocked her and wiped away her tears.
"Mommy, you still love me if me put finger in polenta? Even you tell me get burn?"
"My little explorer, I will always love you, no matter what you do!"

She was extremely happy that her experiment with no-napping in the afternoon succeeded. But later, she dozed off face-down on her salad bowl and never got to play with her friends in the park.

On a very hot summer day, Emma decided to match her silk dress with a wool hat and fur boots, although mother told her she would be hot. She really wanted to know what it means to feel very hot, so she insisted on leaving the house wearing her unusual outfit.

Emma was so hot in the park that she felt suffocated and couldn't even play! She sat on the bench sweating and dizzy until mommy convinced her to at least give up the hat.

In the evening, she said to her mom:
"Y'know that these fur boots not good in the summer. Make ma feet look ugly!"

One day, while mommy was hanging clothes in the balcony and her young brother was brushing the cat with a sand rake, Emma drew a **huge dinosaur** on the wall with crayons that looked very much like an upset piglet

When mommy returned from the balcony, her face turned white; now, one couldn't tell the difference between mommy's complexion and the wall, before Emma painted it with dinosaur.

"Mommy, y'know not me draw here. My hand alone started to draw, me was busy to think about our vacation at seaside!"

"Emma, I don't even know what's worse: that we have to paint the hall or that you've started telling me lies?"

Emma knew that sweets are not very healthy and that you are allowed to eat cakes only on certain days, and only a little amount because otherwise, your stomach hurts and you can become very fidgety and nervous. However, at her friend Mara's party, Emma decided to do another experiment.

So, while mommy was talking to other mothers, Emma crept into the kitchen, opened the fridge, took a plate full of cakes from inside, and ate a lot — that is, about three.

She couldn't eat more than that because she felt very sick to her stomach and ran to her mom to ask for a pill or a belly patch. Since that day, Emma has never eaten more than half a cake.

One summer morning, Emma, her brother and their parents went to a wonderful playground: it was sunny, with lots of pools, slides and colorful ring floats.

They were all playing in the water. There were many children in that place, and Emma had already befriended two other older girls. Seeing that they did not stay very close to their parents, Emma decided she no longer needed her mom and dad, so she moved away from them and ... she got lost.

When she realized that she didn't know how to get back to mommy and daddy, she got really frightened and started screaming and crying.

Luckily, dad had always kept an eye on her and helped her get back to the family. Emma cried a lot in her mother's arms, and after wiping away her tears, she decided, "Me not like get lost, mommy, was not funny at all! Me not do it anymore! Today."

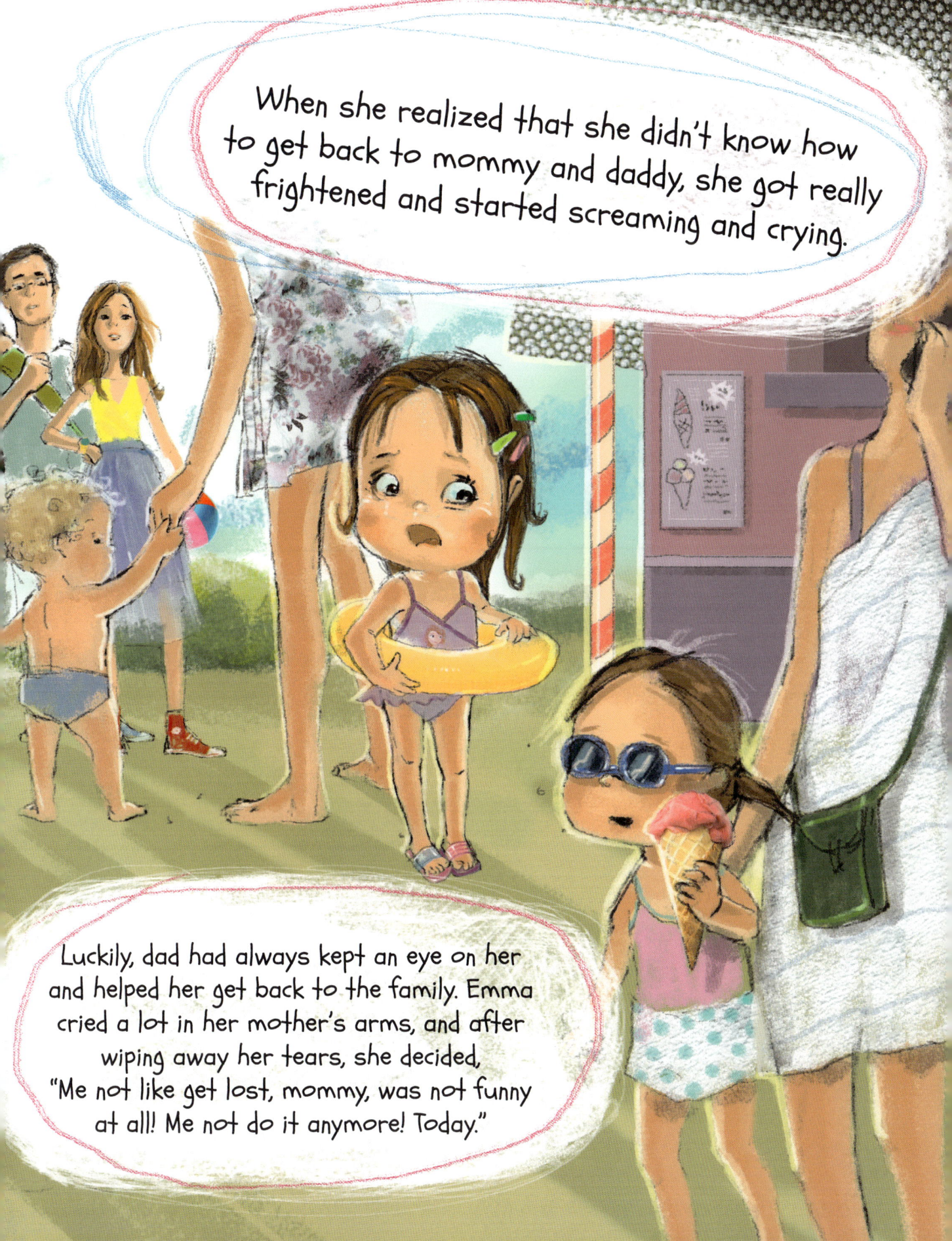

One Sunday afternoon, while Emma and her fluffy brother were getting ready for a bubble bath in the large bathtub, a sudden idea crossed Emma's mind!

How about inviting the cat to their party?

So, she went to pick up the sleeping cat from on top of the radiator and dropped it in the foamy bathtub. The kitten didn't like the diving at all, nor the lavender-scent foam...

... it meowed dissatisfied, threw Emma a reproachful look, and quickly jumped back on the radiator. Displeased, the cat shook off the water from its paws, while small clouds of foam trembled on its whiskers.

Meeoow!

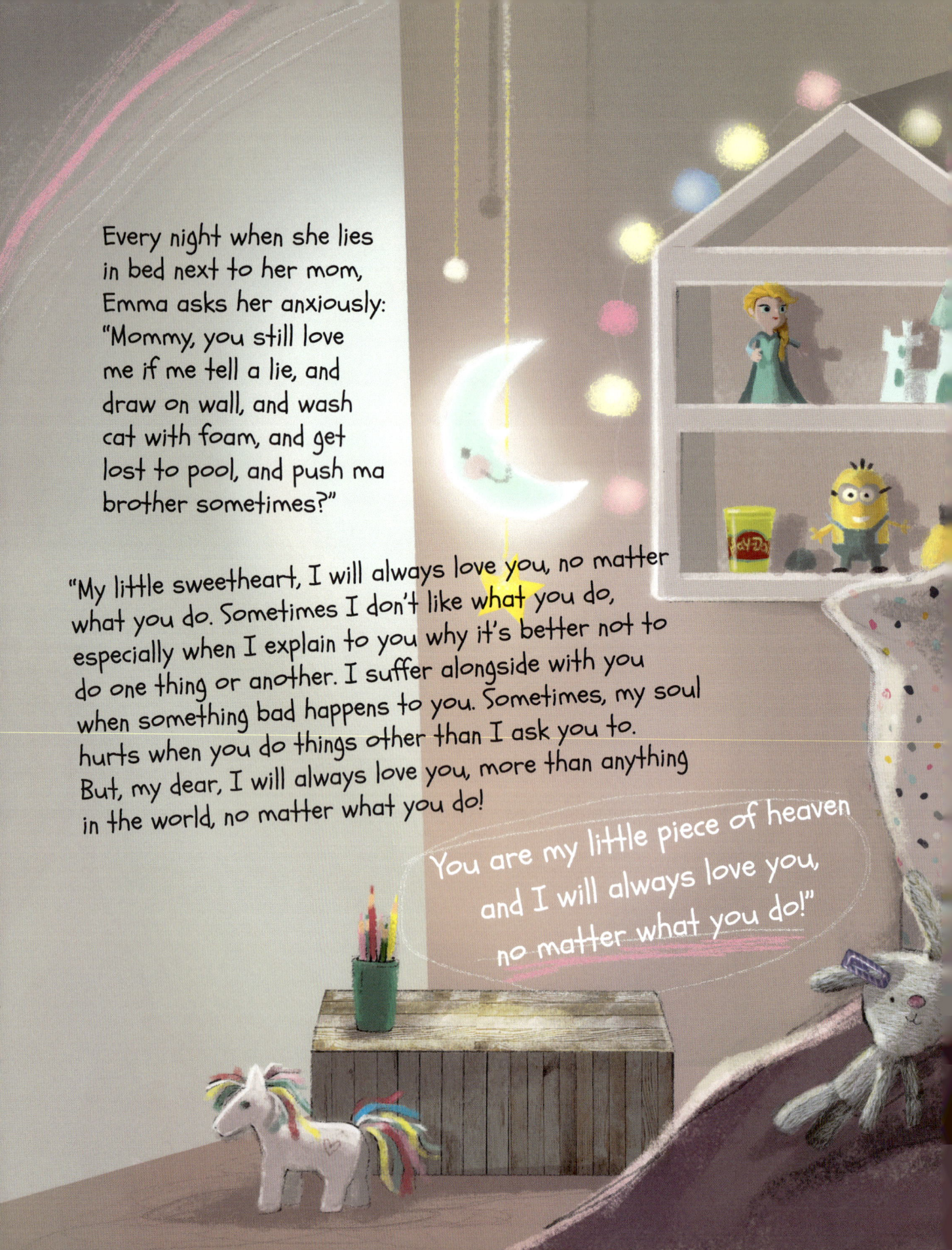

Every night when she lies in bed next to her mom, Emma asks her anxiously: "Mommy, you still love me if me tell a lie, and draw on wall, and wash cat with foam, and get lost to pool, and push ma brother sometimes?"

"My little sweetheart, I will always love you, no matter what you do. Sometimes I don't like what you do, especially when I explain to you why it's better not to do one thing or another. I suffer alongside with you when something bad happens to you. Sometimes, my soul hurts when you do things other than I ask you to. But, my dear, I will always love you, more than anything in the world, no matter what you do!

You are my little piece of heaven and I will always love you, no matter what you do!"

My dears,
I think we adults, have kind of forgotten the joy of the playing,
of the unexpected discoveries. I think we got too used to
our grown-ups outfits and polite smiles.
And, when our children assault us with naughties
that disturb our peace and comfort, instead of enjoying their play,
we are overwhelmed and upset that we have to
sweep the floor, paint the walls, sew the curtain
and dry the puppy with a hair dryer.

I challenge you to learn the lesson of joy
from our children: play more
and do the cleaning together!

Ioana Chicet-Macoveiciuc